i think this feeling is *hope*

hazyn forsythe

i think this feeling is *hope*

Published by hazyn forsythe in 2022

Business Enquiries: hazynforsythe@gmail.com

More Information:

1. Website (Tumblr): https://hazynforsythe.tumblr.com
2. Instagram: @hazynbee and @hazyns

(NB: The links to these sources may be subject to change over time, but are correct at the time of publishing)

Copyright © hazyn forsythe (2022)

All rights reserved, including the rights of hazyn forsythe to be identified as the writer, editor, and creative developer of this work, which have been asserted by them in accordance with Section 77 of the Copyright, Designs, and Patents Act of 1988.

Cover design and photography by hazyn forsythe

HEX codes for covers: #bc6484, #efc9d8, #ffffff

Printed and bound with Ingram Spark

ISBN: 978-1-7396146-0-7

contents

foreword — p.5
acknowledgements — p.17
resources — p.18

2017 — p.21
my mind — 22
embody — 24

2018 — p.26
colour — 27
the things i'll want — 28

2019 — p.31
blue — 32
help her — 34
killer — 35

2020 — p.36
melt — 37
burn — "
piece — 38
spear — "
i fear the day i'll lose you — "

i think this feeling is **hope**

2021

you heard what i said	41
sensation/definitive	"
perspective of past	"
a fearful event	42
entertain	44
time	"
don't let me fall again	45
secrets	46
feel it	"

p.40

2022

this is new	49
bitch	50
speaking up can be frightful	52
fabrication	"
unstuck	53

p.48

i think this feeling is **hope**

foreword *in may 2022*

i've had an eventful few years. as with most people, there was a journey to take between the ages of sixteen and twenty-one. i took my gcses, made it through my a-levels, became an adult, went off to university, studied for three years, and landed where i am now: about to graduate and move towards my master's qualification in creative writing. i've been published amidst my peers in *the abandoned playground*'s '2022 poetry & innovative form student showcase' and taken part in the small-press and anthology project, *monstera*. i'm even working on my own exhibition project to be released into the world in the future.

    however, my career journey wasn't the only one i went through in the past years. it took me a lot to get to where, and who, i am now. in 2017, i was still reeling from the loss of someone close to me and my family just two years before, and from the mental health conditions that were awakened by this look into death's reality. by this time, i was riddled with anxiety that i might experience such loss again, being ruled by obsessive thoughts and

foreword *in may 2022*

compulsive actions that were a desperate attempt to keep anyone – everyone – else from dying or disappearing, too. i had been in and out of therapy for a good few years by this point, but was approaching the most difficult part: accepting that it's okay to let go. to let go of someone important, but also to let go of the tattered threads of control i was grasping onto.

after my previous vent pieces, which had focused on my lack of self-love, my struggles with self-harm, and my confusing relationship with religion (all of which were sparked by a lack of understanding as to why a father would leave his children in favour of a life of addiction), my connection to poetry began to hit its strongest point. it was around this age that i discovered the works of sylvia plath; this incited a revelation within me as i realised that my way of connecting to and expressing my emotions *is* valid and *can* be artistically recognised.

from this point onwards, i allowed myself to befriend poetry not only in my loneliest, emptiest moments but in *every* moment. i told my poems everything, often things i could not bring myself

foreword *in may 2022*

to write down in prose or say out loud. when it got too difficult to tell the story as myself, i wrote about mysterious third-persons or dove into metaphors. this way of connecting to poetry created pieces of more promise than those i'd formed in my earlier years.

    this collection begins with one turning point with 'my mind', a poem i created to work through my fear of allowing myself to begin to heal, and travels with me through several years to another, although no less significant: the point in the story where the protagonist finally gets rewarded with a tale of love. i don't know if this will last forever, but i've come to realise that that's part of the beauty of it... part of the beauty of *life*.

    i've managed to accept what i was struggling to understand at sixteen; not everyone is around forever and that's okay, because every experience i have, every person who walks in and out of my life, and every little moment that passes by is just a small part of what makes life worth it. instead of scrambling about, trying to catch every shard of glass before it falls when a cup breaks in an effort to stop anyone else getting hurt, or – worse –

foreword *in may 2022*

glueing my eyes to every breakable object to stop it ever breaking whilst letting the world pass me by, i'm able to allow a little risk to flood in. it's scary, and i might not be able to keep this connection forever, or this career path stable, or every single person i've ever met alive, but i'm finally able to appreciate the *moments*. i've stopped wrapping my world up in bubble-wrap and praying the air never leaks out of the little, plastic pockets.

    the result? it's fucking terrifying, but i'm experiencing normal, human emotions that i'd been guarded from for years. for decades, even. in early 2021, i proclaimed that i was experiencing happiness for the first time since i was six. i was manic, but i had a point. my life has been messy at best and, through a combination of the wrong medication and shitty coping mechanisms, i had started to view all that mess as something bad. *i must be broken*, i'd thought. *i must be doomed to feel like this forever.* that's where i was wrong. years and years of swirling thoughts and pain even as my loved ones tried to reassure me that yes, i *am* loved had me believing i was the victim of some cruel

*i think this feeling is **hope***

foreword *in may 2022*

fate. in my effort to avoid anything bad happening to everyone around me, i'd completely neglected myself.

this became all the more obvious by 2019, when i went off to university. days before setting off, my parents had found me rocking on my bedroom floor, inconsolable. i viewed the idea of moving away from home as yet another upcoming loss. i would miss so many moments with my family, my school friends, and i'd miss my childhood bedroom which i'd deemed my 'safe space' despite all the shit that occurred within it over the years. the hypothetical sense of emptiness was all too much, and i feared i would not cope; at first, *i didn't.*

despite being almost three years clean by this point, i fell back into self-harm almost the second i was alone. i couldn't see any reasons not to do it as what had stopped me before was the risk of my younger sisters noticing and developing that behaviour, too. even my efforts to look after myself and heal, up to this point, had been for the sake of everyone else. so, without anyone else around to live my life for, i quickly felt empty.

foreword *in may 2022*

this emptiness sent me into toxic friendships from which i'd convinced myself that i did not deserve to escape, even as the tensions grew so thick that these 'friendships' soon exploded themselves. which, of course, left me empty all over again.

eventually, this void began to fill itself with monsters from my past. these were hallucinations that had followed me through from my childhood when i'd first discovered a website full of graphic, adult-rated horror stories and the intense cult-following that had me convinced by the time i hit double-digits that several entities were after me and wanted to do whatever they could to hurt me and everyone i had ever met. with no parents around anymore to convince me that i was protected and no visual, daily proof that my family hadn't been killed and replaced with other creatures (or that they weren't at imminent risk of such a fate), it didn't take long for me to believe the thoughts running through my brain, accepting my delusions and visual, tactile, and audio disturbances as reality.

this caused me to hit a dark point that i hadn't hit since first experiencing the grief i felt in 2015.

i think this feeling is **hope**

foreword *in may 2022*

my world had no clear boundary between reality and fiction and i had no way of knowing what had and hadn't happened to me most of the time. even now, when i look back, there are several empty voids from time i have lost. i rely more than i would like to have to on other people to fill in the gaps for me, but that's something i've had to accept.

i'm aware that, during the rougher episodes of my mental health that pop up every once in a while, i will sometimes become privy to information i usually don't have access to. a memory, or several, will unlock and i don't always have the emotional capability of handling what i've remembered.

by february of 2020, my mental health had hit a monumental low. so, when warnings of a potential worldwide pandemic were given out, my family pulled me home from university in the blink of an eye, soon witnessing firsthand just how far i'd spiralled in the few weeks since the christmas break had ended; i was then set on a path of recovery.

i spent most of my second year of university

foreword *in may 2022*

at home with my family, attending virtual therapy sessions once in a while whilst having my medication levels moved around in just about every possible direction. i talked honestly about what little i *could* remember in my sessions as my doses were tweaked this way and that until we landed on something that worked. the change wasn't exactly instantaneous, but there *were* hints of improvement that kept me going through the flip-flopping emotions and rushing thoughts mixed with a puzzling level of brain fog. i could see that there was another side to my situation, and i hit the point at last where i was able to declare my experience of 'true joy'. it took a little longer to settle into an ability to feel something *other* than joy, but i got there eventually.

    at last, i had the full span of human emotions and was free to return to university in-person; free to experience the world again. i spent the latter part of second year, which i had moved back to lincoln for despite the academic year being less than two months away from finishing, readjusting to what it was to be in society. whilst at home, i had had to shield due to various health conditions

foreword *in may 2022*

within members of my family making them much more at risk than most to the dangers of the big, bad covid-19 that jammed a stick into the gears of many lives; as one could imagine, this alongside my focus on being around family during my mental health recovery deconditioned me from the concept of *people* a fair bit.

 it was scary as hell returning to a place that i knew i had endured pain and yet being an entirely different kind of person at a vastly different point in life to the frightened girl who had stumbled onto campus in 2019. by this time, it was deep into 2021 and the world didn't look how i'd remembered it; shops had plastic shields placed up everywhere you looked, you had to wear a fabric mask on your face to protect both yourself and others from breathing in the dreaded particles, every building you entered had hand-gel dispensers and everyone else suddenly understood the importance of washing their hands. it felt dystopian in many ways, and yet caused me to realise that the behaviours i'd grown up with because of my ocd, which had worsened in 2015 when i got a brutal taste of how high the stakes in

foreword *in may 2022*

life could really be, were now *normal*. cautions i had been bullied for throughout school were now expected of society of a whole, and i felt a little like a secret superhero (especially since, thanks to having been at home for so long to *deal with* my mental health, i now had a much firmer grasp on my emotional responses to things than i used to). i could utilise my in-built caution without letting it be my master.

    i used this – though, at this point i was ready to use just about anything – to build my confidence as i moved towards my third year, formed new friendships, and reignited some that had faltered, and began to put together a circle of people who all trusted each other and whom *i* felt capable of trusting. it was around the end of 2021 that i met my current partner and began to build that relationship. suddenly, all of the poems i'd been writing that year and in the years before about hypothetical connections were challenged by reality; would the real thing pass the test? would it be as good as i had hoped? better? worse?

    throughout the few months of this year, 2022, that have passed now, i have come to experience

foreword *in may 2022*

what romantic love actually feels like. unlike the various false experiences of 'romance' i've had, sprinkled throughout my past, this connection is mutually *good*. i've come to realise that something doesn't have to last forever to have a positive impact on my life, and that i am allowed to enjoy what i am experiencing right now.

whether this lasts forever (which i hope it does) or reaches an ending point in the near or distant future, i know now that every person who enters my life is there for a reason. every single thing, no matter how good or bad they have seemed in each moment, that has happened in my life has built me up to this point. my strength has been tested, i've developed a sense of self-confidence and courage, and i'm being rewarded with the ability to stop and notice how beautiful it all can be.

i am incredibly grateful for every person who has entered my life, no matter how shitty they might have acted or, conversely, how wonderful they may have been, no matter how long their stay.

there is a warmth that spreads through me whenever i think about my future and it's new

foreword *in may 2022*

to me; i'm used to being lorded by fear of what may be to come. now, all i feel is this warmth. it's like the sun is shining from the inside of my heart and spreading out, and i want to let it. i want to let this feeling shine so brightly that it reaches out and warms other people, too.

i think this feeling is *hope.*

acknowledgements *in may 2022*

acknowledgements

thank you to everyone who has stood by me in my journey. to my family, my friends, to the members of educational staff at school and university who listened when i was struggling and pushed me to always try my best. to everyone who reassured me that my best is always good enough. to everyone who pushed and challenged me even when i pushed back harder. to everyone who has had patience and loved me despite how hard i've made it to do so at times. thank you to everyone who has led me to where i am today and encouraged me when i've needed it the most. lastly, thank you to everyone who reads this book and follows me along even one piece of my journey. i value you all.

resources

if you have been impacted by topics contained in this book or would like to find out more, feel free to visit the links below.
i do not own these links; they are each from organisations, charities, and entities beyond myself.

Mind (UK)
https://www.mind.org.uk

NHS (UK)
https://www.nhs.uk/mental-health

YoungMinds (UK)
https://www.youngminds.org.uk

WHO (International)
https://www.who.int/health-topics/mental-health

for more information on my work and creative ventures, see the links on p.2.

i think this feeling is *hope*

hazyn forsythe

*i think this feeling is **hope***

2017

*i think this feeling is **hope***

my mind (2017)

my mind is a prison, trapping me inside,
and it is surrounding me with its lies.

my mind is a labyrinth, there's no clear escape,
but my mind is my own, i should accept this fate.

self-torturing, oppressing, suppressing my dreams,
excruciatingly painful, and yet a part of me.

my mind is crumbling, spiralling, pushing me to madness,
i'm helpless and terrified, save me from this malice.

my mind is a rose bush, my mind is a thorn,
so sweet yet destructive, and so prone to harm.

my mind can be beautiful, and yet incomplete,
it's broken, it's breaking, it's ruining me.

with all these complaints, you'd think i'd seek solace,
or comfort and quiet, in words spoke' with softness.

yet without this hurricane, this wreck of a mind,
i am empty, and soulless, with vices to find.

this anxiety, this stress, this torment, this pain,
filled a crevice created when i felt unsafe.

safe. this fear keeps me so, it makes me be careful,
be cautious, use caution, be oh-just-so mindful.

yet frightened, yet terrified, yet broken, and for what?
to be what i'm used to, as peace i've forgot'.

i want to escape, i don't want this fate, and yet without
control, i do not feel safe.
without these disorders of mind controlling me, i cannot
feel calm, and cannot feel free.

my logic feels backwards, i know, i am sure,
so if one feels confusion, then here i implore,
that reading this passage, one may understand,
that without my madness, i'm not who i am.

help me, for i am sure i cannot help myself,
for now this mind-sickness is my picture of health.

i want to know different, i want to be free,
to have control of my own mind, not it over me.
yet taking that first step – of letting it go,
of freeing that madness – if i can, i don't know.

to do this alone, i doubt it is possible,
but even with help, i could run into trouble.

my mind is many things, but it is not okay,
it is not alright, it won't let me be safe.

so tell me what can i do, to feel some relief,
to kill all my pain, to live out my dreams?

if i pull out the sorrow, fear, and pain from my mind,
what can i fill it with, after loss of one so kind?

i know what were triggers, i know why i'm broken,
but they're issues unfixable by simple words spoken.

my mind is a jail cell, please find me the key,
unlock the hard door, and let me be free.

i think this feeling is **hope**

embody (2017)

with lips so pale that they seem blue

like bruises, injuries,

she's tried and true.

her skin like ice; cold, transparent,

showing veins, and yet no-one

ever saw her pain.

her hair, once golden, now a faint, pale grey;

thin wisps, split ends,

endless frays.

i think this feeling is **hope**

she's beautiful, yet in an uncanny way,

her once bright eyes now have

no soul to display.

her fingers, delicate, may snap like sticks,

yet no-one will be there

to stitch and fix.

recover her beauty,

recover her grace,

please, someone, bring life back to her face.

i think this feeling is **hope**

2018

*i think this feeling is **hope***

colour (2018)

pink cheeks, blushing roses
innocent girl, she always poses
she's always pretending
that she's so pure
like her head isn't flooding with guts and gore

blue rushing water – from her sink
as she takes a minute to breathe, and think
her breath grows heavy,
she's tired now
wondering if she can be fixed somehow

red mind knows so much more –
her other mind is a filthy whore –
thinks thoughts so lusting
she begs for death
but knows her time isn't over yet

green gardens, growing trees
all she wants is harmony...
but her eyes are heavy,
and she's so weak
her mind acts without apology

purple pills, and hospital beds...
they finally got a look into her head
and as they realised, their hearts filled with dread
at the fact that, for a moment,
she had wanted to be dead.

i think this feeling is **hope**

the things i'll want (2018)

i'll climb up to the top of your funfair ride
if you promise that i won't get trapped inside
those pretty hands;
a cage, my cell
please don't become my own personal hell.

i'll give you my heart if you spare me the details
and protect me just like a delicate seashell
call me pretty, and call me sweet
but don't trample me beneath your feet.

and in return, my heart will yearn
and i'll love you more than anything on this earth
i'll trust you with everything if you keep me safe
but know of my independence and please have faith.

i may be weak but i have some strength too
i have double standards, i know i do.

treat me right, and for a while,
it's you i'll adore
but eventually, with guilt,
i'll find you a bore.

*i think this feeling is **hope***

but hurt me, break me, and i'll stick like glue
i don't want to be like this but such is true.

i'm damaged goods, a ruined commodity, but either way
i hope you'll love me
and treat me well
even if i don't deserve it
and maybe, just maybe, make me believe i'm worth it.

*i think this feeling is **hope***

i think this feeling is **hope**

2019

*i think this feeling is **hope***

blue (2019)

hi.
my brain is on a landslide
& i hope that you don't mind
if i go out of my mind

    hi.
    everything is changing
    and this state that my brain's in
    could be pretty... bad

        i don't know if i'm ready
        don't know that i like this
        i'm feeling unsteady

                help me?

        why am i tumbling?
        i just keep falling
        deeper and deeper and further and further
        into this dangerous place,
        this unhelpful state

how do i get out?

        "get out of bed,
        you'll become depressed"
        i think i'm already there

            i should be excited
            but instead i'm just frightened
            i shouldn't be like this
            but it won't go away

i think this feeling is **hope**

i feel heavy
i'm really not ready
sometimes i'm happy, but
that doesn't last all day

    so goodbye,
    i guess,
    i'm still leaving home
    and there's this weight on my chest
    but by now i know that life won't give me a rest
    is this some kind of test?

              will i be okay?

        it's happening
        like every year
        but, unlike before, i won't be here

            i won't be home
            i won't feel safe
            at least that's what
            my thoughts say

                "it's exhausting"
                "stop worrying"
                well, yeah, i'm tired too
                if i knew how to stop it,
                that's what i'd do

    ...wouldn't you?

                if only you knew
                what i go through
                that my pain, i guess,
                is true

          and i feel
        kind of
          blue.

i think this feeling is **hope**

help her (2019)

the tyres that tire
the road beneath
again and again
each day, each week
bring her further and further
from safety, from peace
and why – oh why – must she
feel so weak?
given no choice but to face defeat
unable to scream, unable to speak
unable to run with these ties on her feet
unable to fight
only able to cry
only able to lay there
stuck, and wondering: "why?"
wondering if, and when, and how soon
she'll die
wondering if there will even be anything
left of her to find
is this her last night?
was happiness a lie?
a rarity left only for few to find?
or will she continue with life?
but scared, perhaps *wishing* to die?

this all isn't right
if only someone could save her from this plight,
or give her chance to fight,
some kind of hope; some light
and free her tonight,
somehow make it alright, but–
but there's no hope in sight.

i think this feeling is **hope**

killer (2019)

watch me blend into the floor,
a body, a corpse,
lights flicker as i snigger,
i'm waiting for more.
an opportunity to appear,
to do something so queer –
as to rip out one's brain
from inside their ear.
and their bones?
well i'll break them
snap them up like kit-kat sticks.
nothing can stop me
from playing out my tricks.
unaware, in they'll wander
come here to your doom.
i bet you didn't expect
to die quite so soon.
carelessness makes me ponder –
but i don't like to think –
why they're all just so stupid,
so now down they'll all sink.
watch them blend into the floor,
they're all dead, of course.
the carpet is red now,
it's not grey anymore.

i think this feeling is **hope**

2020

*i think this feeling is **hope***

melt (2020)

now, if only you knew
the way my breath shakes
when our eyes meet –
is it too late?

we're forbidden,
but – fuck it – i'm smitten
your eyes melt me
they're a hot-chocolate abyss

i sink into the thought…
what if we kissed?
would you understand
how long i've longed to hold your hand?

but you're no man

burn (2020)

dawn's break
the time we shared together was brief but brilliant
the first glimpse of the rising sun

a splash of colour burned into my mind
once coal, now the ocean
the flame flickered then s p u t t e r e d out

i think this feeling is hope

piece (2020)

broken glass
blades of grass
cut f r e s h

spear (2020)

your garden's roses scream, juliet.
they tell me of your nightmares, your soul stole' by a man.
you chase the forbidden only when it's known to you
burned hearts bleed blue

why risk it for a montague?
desire will be thy death.

i fear the day i'll lose you (2020)

forever is such a long time, it encompasses everything under the sun, every prize left to be won, so much that it carries such weight, breaking into the realm of things we can't help but take for granted, until

in an instant we lose that forever, that promise of eternity, and
time becomes meaningless when she's not here with me.

*i think this feeling is **hope***

i think this feeling is **hope**

2021

*i think this feeling is **hope***

you heard what i said (2021)

and from blistered feet comes a blistered soul
why not shove it into the coffin?
and the bruises beat the marks from the teeth
when the jaw decides to lock in

sensation/definitive (2021)

yearning; lust tears at my heart
learning; something i'd ought to start
earning; what's my place in this world?
churning; my stomach, it swirls

perspective of past (2021)

obsessed with perfection
accuracy
injury to mirror fictional injury
       s
            p
                  i
           r
                 a
                      l

i think this feeling is **hope**

a fearful event (2021)

i don't want to.
the world fried my brain and
its fingers are clawing out again.
the static is buzzing and filling my mind
with thoughts from people i left behind...
the darkness rises inside me.
it knows how to hurt me.
it will do it again.

again, again, again.
over and over.
my flesh suit wanders without purpose
without warning or thought.
and, each time i wake up,
it leaves me distraught.

i came back.
back to the place where the voices scream
where i'm reminded of a world so mean
but the memories aren't inside of me

    where is my brain?

all i remember is the fear and the pain.
promises broken all over again
am i going insane?
no, i did that already.

    but why is the world so fucking heavy?

i think this feeling is **hope**

when will i know the freedom of peace?
i thought that god would have given it to me
baptised somewhere between pre-teen and teen
i thought my soul was clean

does jesus love me?

what does he know that i don't?
are there lies i told, promises i broke?
my lungs are about to collapse from the smoke
but it isn't mine
the world left it behind

they
fried my mind
and now we're on
a chopping block

when will the nightmares stop?

my voice begins to drop
quieter, quieter,
what if others forgot?
would they notice if i went silent, or not?

i think this feeling is **hope**

entertain (2021)

for a happily ever after
would you sail the seven seas?
would you dissipate into the air to
become the air i breathe?

and i'd let it out through laughter
if you'd swirl for a moment by me
distract me, dear girl, from this rotten world
and seep into the blood i bleed

time (2021)

the snow feels so far away
when you're watching it through the window
as the children, they dance and play,
and you wonder, "where did my life go?"
last i knew it was may,
and the spring was fading so soon
summer is the time when the sun bleeds,
no more snow to melt into dew

i think this feeling is **hope**

don't let me fall again (2021)

fuck
one of the words i feared
we all know it rhymes with duck and luck
yet it's sharper than a spear

shit
another spiral of terror
you'll be like him if you slip, cut those delicate wrists
bleed mistakes onto the platter

bitch
you don't matter; follow the pattern
these words i have always known

fuck, **shit**, and **bitch**
now i'll start to itch
he's controlling my mind again

i think this feeling is **hope**

secrets (2021)

secrets climb walls
they skitter around, searching for entrances
little holes where they can start to spill out

secrets clamber along recklessly
their one goal to shatter what existed before
they know how to cause ruin

secrets slither in
every crack and crevice in your body contains a secret
they tangle themselves around your gut, making you feel sick

there are secrets in your blood.

feel it (2021)

they know i'd do it, too
take scalds from winter mornings
hold lashes inside me, tight
but who does that help?

if the day comes
that i must prove my worth
i'll not go gently

i think this feeling is **hope**

i think this feeling is **hope**

2022

*i think this feeling is **hope***

this is new (2022)

i only expected darkness from the world
shadows, demons, they haunted me once
told me i was not worth anything good.

but times have changed and so have i
i think this feeling is hope; it's strange,
unusual to feel so comfortable, so safe.

but what of permanence?
what if they leave?
so used to abandonment, i don't remember —

trust.
i want to try, though...
i think i might be good for them, and they're surely good for me.

sunset shines on their cheeks...
a smile that hides from the camera
things only seen by me.

*i think this feeling is **hope***

bitch (2022)

did you not know that i am strong?
we did many things together
several 'wrong', at least to me
but i'm sure you loved them...
you loved the activities, the control,
sit. stop. drop. roll.
i was never your dog, and yet
you teased me with the treat of
attention, a break from loneliness,
if i only followed your command.

i never wanted to kiss you.
you're not my type. no-one like you is.
why did you long so deeply to keep
your fingers tangled in my hair,
around my throat, in a leash?
let go of me... please.
i never pleased you, and yet
i always did? i always did what you:
said. wanted. demanded. threatened.
i must only listen.

i think this feeling is **hope**

but when is it my turn? even now,
i lie in wait. what will you want from me
next? but then, i remember, i'm not
yours anymore. you never loved me. i'm
loved by someone better now. they
love me? somehow, i have
found everything. everything i wanted,
needed, dreamed about. it is wonderful.

i finally know love. not what it is to be
some pet, some pathetic spawn.
i'm so happy!

so why, i ask, do i still feel your
grip? the ghost of a hand, the blood
that drips. but did i ever bleed? or merely
imagine it? i cannot remember and
i hate that i am so forever stuck.
without memories or context, alone, and dead.
let me out of your world. don't make me beg.

i think this feeling is **hope**

speaking up can be frightful (2022)

let me be disrespectful
allow me to drive a rift into the
blood that ties this creation
together. i know you
feel the need to keep the
peace, but just as i
stumble, our knowledge breaks
this bond apart.

fabrication (2022)

i don't know how to write something happy
i'm used to stories where everything bleeds
holes tear open
breathe, then drip
this is a new feeling to me
to be sewn together by love
i didn't know what that was like before their arrival
their debut within me

i think this feeling is **hope**

unstuck (2022)

i've finally freed the glue from my fingers,
it's peeled off, rolled into little balls that i've
discarded in the bin.

i've finally detached these threads from my skin;
they'd pulled me together in a crumpled knot,
ready to fall to pieces but unable
to scream.
unable to smash, or float, or flutter down.

sometimes it's okay to hit the ground.

the ground is designed to stand on, after all; gravity
exists so that we may fall once in a while.

and that's okay

i don't have to hang from the ceiling, watching from above but never living, some sick spider caught in its own silky web.

be free, little spider

go see where the world can take you

live a little,

i'm going to.

i think this feeling is **hope**

i think this feeling is ***hope***